AN ERST OF BEES

A WILD ALPHABET OF
COLLECTIVE NOUNS

For Monee, who started the stories.
—S. S.

For Gretchen and Eric, who believed.
—L. P.

For Priya and Jaeda, who inspire. In memory of Grammy Donna.
—D. L.

Special thanks to our technical and support team:
Tom Few, Nathan Smalara, FX, Stratis Kakadelis and Regina Kakadelis.

Visit us at www.SquirrelHousePublishing.com
Email: TheSquirrel@SquirrelHousePublishing.com

Printed in the United States of America

ISBN: 1523864397
ISBN-13: 978-1523864393

AN ERST OF BEES

A WILD ALPHABET OF COLLECTIVE NOUNS

Written by Susan Smalara and Lisa Pifer

Illustrated by Deni Laskey Few

Collective Noun

: a noun that names a group of people or things

Army of Frogs

Leaping and swimming are sport for a frog.
Sometimes they bask in the sun on a log.

Business of Ferrets

These nocturnal ferrets sleep during the day,
Then when the sun sets they hunt and they play.

Crash of Rhinoceroses

Some rhinos have two horns, some rhinos have one.
Most of the rhinos weigh over a ton.

Drift of Hogs

Watch the hogs snuffle, their snouts to the ground.
They're pleasantly plump and their tails curl around.

Erst of Bees

Bees work to turn nectar into a treat.
They make golden honey…it tastes sugar sweet!

Family of Sardines

With a bright flash of silver, sardines swim in schools.
They prefer the deep ocean to shallow sea pools.

Gaggle of Geese

Geese honk as they land near the edge of a lake.
They're looking for food and a well-deserved break.

Husk of Jackrabbits

Racing by at fast speeds and bounding so high,
These large-footed hares are quite agile and spry.

Intrigue of Kittens

Curious creatures who like to have fun,
These kittens explore when their naptime is done.

Jar
of
Nuthatches

Climbing so
nimbly head
first down the
tree,
the nuthatch
will find what
the others
can't see.

Knot of Toads

Toads have short legs and they like to walk.
A deep throaty croak is how the males talk.

Leap of Leopards

Leopards are cunning
and powerful
creatures.
The spots on their
coats are a camouflage
feature.

Mob of Kangaroos

These kangas hop forward at very fast speeds,
With a tail used for steering and strong legs indeed.

Nest of Crocodiles

Lazily resting are these crocodiles.
You'd better beware; don't be fooled by their smiles.

Ostentation of Peacocks

Proudly the peacocks strut over the ground.
When their tail feathers fan, colors abound.

Pod of Whales

Whales like to spyhop, their heads to the sun,
Splashing and playing, they're looking for fun.

Quiver of Cobras

The cobras rear up when reacting to fright.
A menacing hood flare means
they may bite.

Rabble
of
Butterflies

When butterfly
wings so softly
unfold,
their shimmering
hues are a sight
to behold.

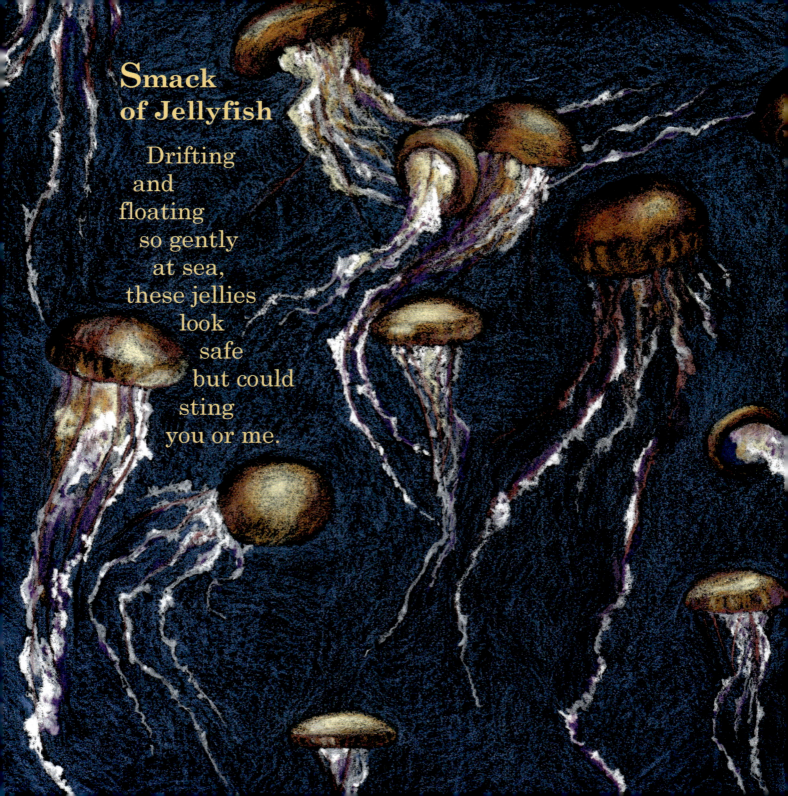

Smack
of Jellyfish

Drifting
and
floating
so gently
at sea,
these jellies
look
safe
but could
sting
you or me.

Tower of Giraffes

The long-necked giraffe can stand nineteen feet tall.
No other land animal comes close at all.

Unkindness of Ravens

Clever and keen are these inky black birds,
And the caw of these ravens can often be heard.

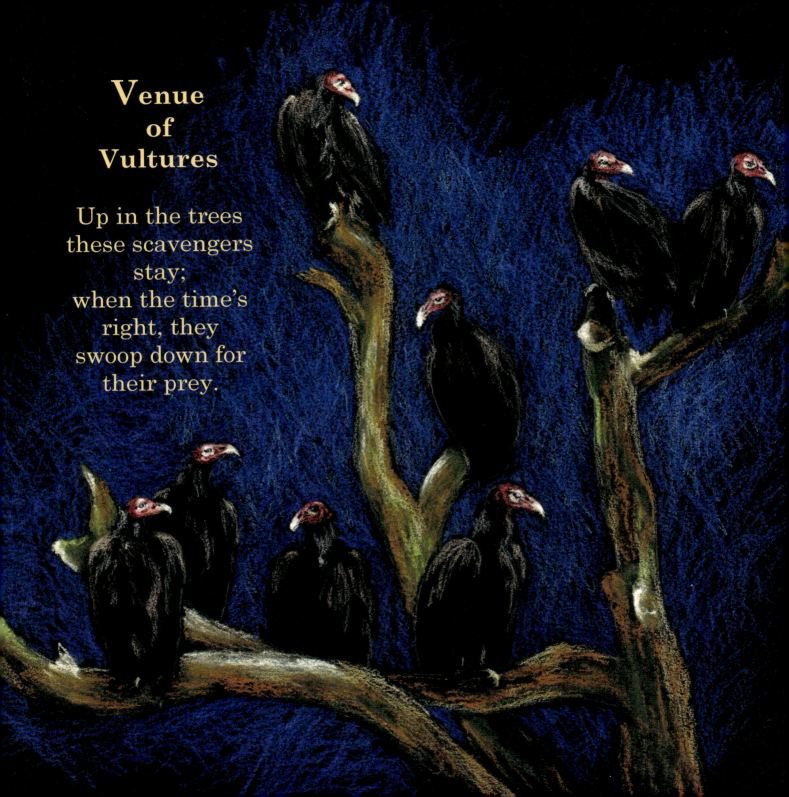

Venue of Vultures

Up in the trees
these scavengers
stay;
when the time's
right, they
swoop down for
their prey.

Whoop of Gorillas

Male silverbacks are the big ones in charge.
When challenged they're noisy and look very large.

EXaltation of Larks

Bursting with song, the larks fly so high.
Spreading their wings, they fill up the sky.

Yoke of Oxen

Look at the oxen so hardy and strong.
They work as a team, all the day long.

Zeal of Zebras

With a kick of their heels and a toss of their manes,
These black and white zebras gallop the plains.

More Wild Collective Nouns

Bed of Clams
Brood of Hens
Charm of Hummingbirds
Cloud of Gnats
Colony of Beavers
Drove of Donkeys
Flock of Sheep
Gaze of Raccoons
Kettle of Hawks
Leash of Foxes
Lounge of Lizards
Pack of Dogs
Parade of Elephants
Plague of Locusts
Prickle of Hedgehogs
Pride of Lions
School of Fish
Shiver of Sharks
Sleuth of Bears
Sneak of Weasels
Tribe of Goats
Wisdom of Wombats

Made in the USA
Middletown, DE
10 November 2019